# Welcome

*To an H&A full of design inspiration*

Here at *Homes & Antiques*, we love the real homes that we feature so much that we've put 25 of our favourites into this special edition, which is split into five chapters covering everything from vintage crafty to 20th-century style. Each chapter has a handy get-the-look section at the end too.

When we're deciding which homes to feature in the magazine every month, we always question what a *Homes & Antiques* house is and the short answer is: it's one where the owners show real creativity, initiative and flair.

Our owners come from all walks of life and they're aged from their mid-twenties to their seventies and beyond. Their houses can be modern or traditional, in the city or country, but they have two uniting factors: firstly, the homes are curated and have evolved over time; and, secondly, the owners have a love and appreciation of beautiful design and objects from every era.

This makes for a fantastically eclectic selection, from the airy, open-plan eco conversion (on p46) to a former pub that has been converted to a family home – and that also boasts one of the UK's smallest cinemas (on p12).

We hope you enjoy this mix of houses and if you're not already familiar with – or want to find out more about – *Homes & Antiques*, please see our subscription offer on page 128.

Finally, if you have a home that you'd like to see in our pages, please drop us a line. We're always on the lookout for something just that bit different!

*Angela*

Angela Linforth
Editor, *Homes & Antiques*

54

24

127

# Contents

# Vintage crafty

*From flea-market finds to handmade accessories, everything in these homes has a story to tell*

**KATIE HALLETT,**
HOMES EDITOR

**Beautiful vintage textiles** sporting bright floral motifs have been used in these homes to create wonderfully jolly – and unique – interiors. Unsurprisingly, the homeowners are all rather handy with a needle-and-thread: nattily covering everything from cushions to junk shop-bought headboards and dining chairs in their enviable collection of fabrics (rummaged for at vintage fairs, naturally). Despite the similarity in style between the interiors, the homes range from a 16th-century thatched cottage to a 1980s townhouse and even a former coaching inn that now contains a 32-seat cinema, showing just how adaptable the look is. All that's required is a tenacious hunter-gather instinct.

# Treasures from a lifetime

*Jenny Warner has a love of bright colours and bold pattern, as her coastal home in Southsea shows...*

FEATURE **KATIE HALLETT** PHOTOGRAPHS **RACHEL WHITING**

**FACING PAGE** 'I love my old Sunny Southsea Ices sign, which I bought from a local junk shop. It has wonderful graphics and I like the link with local history.' says homeowner Jenny Warner **THIS PAGE** The dining room has been furnished with junk-shop finds, bought around 25 years ago. 'The Victorian table cost just £80. It was used as a workbench for decades. We turned the top over and used it upside-down,' says Jenny

**LEFT** As in most rooms, the fireplace in the living room is original. 'The Edwardian tiles are a bit battered but then they are 100 years old!' says Jenny **TOP** Fabrics and coffee pots are displayed in the workroom **ABOVE** Jenny and Bronte created a patchwork wall using mismatched wallpaper

For someone who, on seeing the new home her partner had ear-marked for their family, started crying and then reasoned 'nevermind – we can move again,' Jenny Warner has done well. In fact, she and her partner Dom are still enjoying the makeover process over a decade later. 'I change my mind a lot and it's all just too easy to tweak rooms with fresh paint,' says Jenny.

The couple started their coastal house hunt in Whitstable and then worked their way around the south coast until they eventually reached Southsea, where Dom found this property, a four-minute walk from the seafront. The family were in within three months and Jenny and Dom spent endless evenings after tearing off wallpaper and ripping up carpets. 'The house hadn't been decorated in about 20 years – underneath the shag pile we found leopard-print carpet and, under that, lino,' explains Jenny.

Jenny and Dom aren't finished yet though. Along with designs to fit a new kitchen – 'we can't decide whether to go for an ultra-modern or salvaged look' – plans are also afoot to transform the living room with a 1950s Ercol sofa, inky blue paint on the fireplace and oak floorboards. 'It's long overdue. Dom chose the scheme after we moved in and the girls and I have never warmed to it,' says Jenny. 'He would be happier if every room had next to nothing in it apart from one amazing chair.' Needless to say, Jenny doesn't quite share this view.

Throughout the house, brightly coloured ceramics, highly patterned fabrics and hundreds of books by the early 19th-century company Blackie & Son adorn surfaces, while bold posters and wallpapers make walls pop. 'This stuff didn't appear overnight, it's a lifetime thing,' says Jenny. Bronte has my diary from the 1970s and I would rave about my collections even then. My problem is that I don't discriminate – I like everything. It all happens by accident too, so unfortunately it's a bit of a jumble.' We beg to differ. For any lover of vintage (or second-hand, as Jenny calls it), her home – and especially her multi-coloured workroom – is a joy. Some items have been kept since childhood or given to her by her sisters and many were found for pence at car boot sales. 'It's staggering what I've found – I can never understand why people sell things for so little!' ∎
*To find out more about Jenny's collections, visit her blog at thecustards.blogspot.co.uk*

*'This stuff didn't appear overnight, it's a lifetime thing. Bronte has my diary from the 1970s and I would rave about my collections even then'*

**CLOCKWISE FROM TOP LEFT** 'The patchwork quilt was just £8 from a charity shop a couple of years ago – it was in a carrier bag with about 100 extra patches, which I used to make a cushion from,' says Jenny; Jenny loves making items from vintage fabrics. 'The girls and I often sit in the work room, chatting, sewing or using the computer'; the garden chairs were bought from a junk shop in Dulwich and have been recovered by Jenny many times; the bold, colourful theme is continued in Bronte's bedroom, which the couple fitted with velux windows

# A house of surprises

*This former pub in a small Somerset town has been lovingly restored into a family home, complete with library and vintage-style cinema*

FEATURE **KATIE HALLETT** PHOTOGRAPHS **JASON INGRAM**

**LEFT** Juliet Maclay lives here with her husband, David. Together they run The Roxy cinema, which is on the ground floor of the house **THIS PAGE** 'David based the design of the library on the panelled rooms of the early 18th century that he was familiar with from growing up in New England,' says Juliet

'I've always loved the ordinary stuff that most people throw away. As a result, our home isn't full of valuable antiques but we do have some quirky treasures'

**CLOCKWISE FROM TOP LEFT** The kitchen is in what was the public bar. The sink was found in an Italian market and was originally used for the cleaning and preparation of fish; 'The Georgian desk in the guest bedroom was my grandfather's and I love its wonkiness and simplicity,' says Juliet; the Gallé cat in the bar belonged to Juliet's grandmother; the Roxy's 32 seats are from Bristol's Colston Hall

**THIS PAGE** 'I found the guest room bed in a junk shop in France and reupholstered it using remnants of old Welsh blankets gleaned from vintage fairs over the years,' says Juliet **RIGHT** The office suite in Juliet's study was found online and was made by Fortuna in the 1950s **BELOW RIGHT** Decanters and bottles from car boot sales decorate the bathroom. The map is the original London Underground diagram before it was redesigned in 1933

W e've featured homes that are run as businesses before, but this house in Axbridge with its own cinema is an *H&A* first. And we're not just talking about a home cinema. The Roxy is a fully functioning, 32-seat affair with its own box office and bar. The foyer – decorated in hot pinks and punchy reds – was inspired by a 1920s cinema in Amsterdam, while the bar is all 1950s primary colours. Needless to say, it's not the sort of thing you'd expect to stumble across in a quiet Somerset market town.

Juliet and David Maclay bought the property – a Georgian coaching inn – when, Juliet admits, it was in the sort of state that would make most people run a mile. 'The upper floors were divided into B&B accommodation, while the ground floor had functioned as The Lion pub for over 250 years.' But the Maclays loved the idea of moving into a place they could truly make their own.

After living for years without space to properly display their books, the first room the Maclays created – somewhat unusually – was the library, with its beautiful Georgian-style shelving and panelling. 'David built it, combining two rather depressing bed-and-breakfast rooms from the original inn,' says Juliet. Since then, the couple have been gradually working through the house and garden which, when they moved in, was a concrete car park.

Ten years after moving into the house, the family decided to create one of the smallest cinemas in Britain. They had puzzled over what to do with the former coach entrance and eventually found the answer in its gently sloping floor and the

fact that it is completely underground. 'The slope meant we couldn't use it as a living area so we started joking that we could turn it into a cinema,' explains Juliet. 'I spent two years looking for seats and was ready to give up on the idea when a friend was walking past Bristol's Colston Hall and saw its post-war theatre seats piled into a skip. The staff said we were welcome to them, and so The Roxy began.'

The creation of The Roxy offered Juliet – a self-confessed hoarder – the opportunity to bring her extensive collection of vintage fabrics and curiosities into play. 'Because the building has been altered over the centuries we haven't been tied to one particular style, which is perfect for me as I love mixing eras,' she says. 'Creating a 1930s-inspired foyer, 1940s cinema and 1950s bar has allowed us to showcase all the finds that we've gathered over the years.' By finds, she means such gems as the vintage textiles that adorn the bar stools and chairs (left behind from the pub days) and a set of 1920s glass mirror doors that were bought 10 years ago from Wells Trading Post.

The finds aren't exclusive to the cinema though – 'I've always loved the ordinary stuff that most people throw away and, as a result, our home isn't full of valuable antiques but we do have some quirky treasures,' she says. Quirky treasures are thoroughly appropriate for a house that's all about the unexpected: even the kitchen was designed around a 1930s fish preparation sink. 'These things bring the past to life in a way that expensive artwork can't. Well, that's my excuse for having a house full of junk!' laughs Juliet. ∎

*To find out more about The Roxy, visit axbridgeroxy.org.uk*

# Passion for design

*Vintage finds, original art and inherited treasures
combine to make Pippa Connelly's Hampshire cottage
a family home full of warmth and colour*

FEATURE **MAGGIE STEVENSON** PHOTOGRAPHS **JASON INGRAM**

**CLOCKWISE FROM TOP LEFT** Pippa made the cushion covers from new and vintage fabrics; 'I'm always happy if I'm making something'; the blue and white jug is by Burleigh; 'This chair cost £25 from a car boot sale. I painted the legs then covered it in this print from the "Delphina" collection by Harlequin,' says Pippa; at the centre of Pippa's pottery display is a dazzling plate the couple bought in Tuscany **FACING PAGE** The gilt-framed mirror is from Lots Road Auctions and was the first antique that James and Pippa bought together

**THIS PAGE** Bell's bed is piled with cushions sewn by Pippa. Wine boxes were screwed to the wall to create shelves and the curtain was made simply by fixing curtain rings to an ikat throw **FACING PAGE, TOP LEFT** The muted colours and floral fabrics ensure a calm country feel in the bedroom **TOP RIGHT** The washstand in the bathroom previously belonged to James's grandmother **BOTTOM RIGHT** The Victorian dressing table mirror was a gift from James's parents

*'Don't rush. Take time to get to know your home. You need to live in a house to understand how the light and atmosphere changes in each room '*

Pippa Connelly seems to have the work-life balance just right. Living in an idyllic corner of Hampshire, the cottage she shares with her husband James and their two children, Bell and Will, is a relaxed family home and the base for Pippa's soft furnishings business.

The couple migrated from London in stages, moving first to Surrey before settling near the old village of Liphook. The cottage they bought was built as a bungalow in the 1930s but has since been extended and replanned. 'Its quirkiness appealed to me,' says Pippa. 'I could imagine us living there.'

The advice Pippa lives by and encourages her clients to follow is, 'Don't rush. Take time to get to know your home. You need to live in a house and see it through the seasons to understand how the light and atmosphere change in each room.' Pippa discovered that some rooms were apt to feel a little dark in winter, so the couple chose to decorate with pale colours. Cream walls in the kitchen and rose-tinted paint in the bedroom create warmth and light.

These neutral tones also make a good background for the collection of prints, paintings and other artworks that Pippa and James have inherited or received as gifts. The picture that hangs above their bed is a collage made by a creative friend who pieced the entire work from fragments of paper. Elsewhere hangs a group of samplers, stitched by James's mother to mark special family occasions. 'My mother-in-law is a skilled needlewoman and her samplers are a lasting celebration of our wedding and the births of our children', says Pippa. 'They are the things that make a home.'

Antique markets and fairs are a rich source of materials and inspiration for Pippa where she often picks up vintage fabrics, pottery and small items of furniture. 'I love the buzz of walking around an antiques fair. You meet all kinds of interesting people,' she says. 'I was brought up in a home filled with antiques and pictures and my parents-in-law are surrounded by them, too. Collecting and creating are very much in our family.' ∎

**THIS PAGE** The kitchen had already been modernised before the family moved in. Bunting and a Cath Kidston curtain in front of the washing machine keep things pretty **FACING PAGE** 'We bought the standard lamp from Bridport Street Market and I re-covered the shade with vintage fabric,' says homeowner Helen Pinnington. For a trim, try VV Rouleaux

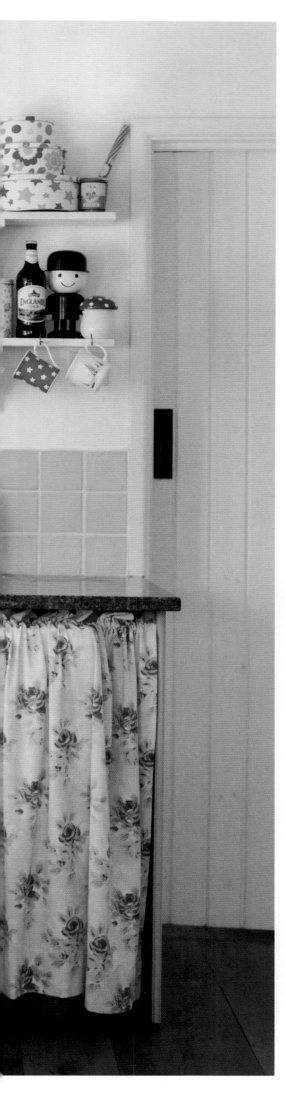

# Vintage revival

*For Helen Pinnington, partner Andy and stepson Harry, an idyllic thatched cottage in Somerset provides the perfect spot for a weekend hideaway*

FEATURE **KATIE HALLETT** PHOTOGRAPHS **BILL KINGSTON**

Dressed in a fabulous 1940s frock and with the ability to bake a mean Victoria sponge (as well as rustle up a perfectly stitched cushion cover from fragile 1950s barkcloth fabric), Helen Pinnington is something of a vintage aficionado. The word 'vintage' is hot property at the moment but for Helen it's not just about embracing a trend, as the briefest glance around her and partner Andy's weekend home shows. The kitchen dresser reveals a lifelong love for 1930s Carlton Ware ceramics; bookshelves are stacked with faded bindings; and Forties and Fifties fabrics adorn cushions, beds and lampshades. 'I've always loved old things,' says Helen. 'When I was about 10, I bought an old eiderdown at a sale – I adored it but the leaking feathers drove my mum mad!' she says.

Four years ago, after spending numerous weekends travelling from their house in London to West Dorset, staying in B&Bs and exploring coastal towns, Helen and Andy decided it made sense to find a holiday home in the area. They were after somewhere with period charm but that didn't need any work – this was to be a place for relaxation. Six months later, after following a recommendation for a pub in a Somerset village, they stumbled across the thatched Lilac Cottage. The cottage was perfect: a 16th-century Grade II-listed building, which just required a good scrub.

In London, Helen and Andy's house is quite modern in feel. In their country home though, Helen was able to indulge in the whole vintage look. 'We had six months between first seeing the cottage and getting the keys, so we spent many weekends in between scouring boot sales for furniture,' she says. Doing things thriftily was always a priority and so, when it came to soft furnishings, Helen turned to her long-neglected sewing machine. Curtains, eiderdowns, bunting and dozens of colourful cushions were created from vintage fabrics found at fairs. She posted images of her creations on her blog and, encouraged by the positive response, decided to begin selling pieces at the Vintage & Handmade Fair in Chipping Sodbury in May 2009.

So what does Andy make of all those florals? 'He just likes the fact that most things in the cottage are vintage or antique. He appreciates things that are British or handmade and would much rather buy old than new,' says Helen. 'When we met, I was working in the city as a lawyer and was living in quite a modern-looking flat. It took us a while to discover our mutual love for all things vintage.'

Weekends are spent visiting Bridport, eating fish and chips in Lyme Regis, or closer to home: walking the neighbour's dog, bird-watching or going to a local car-boot sale. And during trips to steam railway events and fairs, the family can be found donning their vintage finest. 'Life in the 1940s and 1950s was much more refined – men would always be in shirt and tie and women looked so smart, with perfect hair and red lipstick,' says Helen. 'It's a lifestyle that Andy and I hanker after and recreating it is much more achievable here at the cottage.' ■

*To view Helen's blog, go to henhousehomemade.blogspot.com*

'*Curtains, eiderdowns, bunting and dozens of colourful cushions were created from vintage fabrics found at fairs* '

**TOP** Cowboys are a theme in Harry's room **LEFT** Weekends at the cottage are made for relaxing **FAR LEFT** Bunting, a railway poster and ship in a bottle create a cheery feel in the bathroom **FACING PAGE, CLOCKWISE FROM TOP LEFT** The Smeg fridge and the dresser were both found on eBay; the couple's antique bed frame was tricky to manoeuvre into the petite cottage. 'My dad and Andy had to climb up ladders outside and push it in through the bedroom window, while my mum and I pulled it in from the inside!' says Helen; the chairs in the dining room were all bought from boot sales and came to just £10

**THIS PAGE** The cross-stitch sampler to the left of the living room fireplace was made by Janice, the twig deer's head is from Hobby Craft and the 1930s flower painting was from a charity shop **FACING PAGE** Homeowner Janice Issitt sits in her conservatory, which doubles up as her workroom

# An eclectic mix

Inherited collections, thrifty vintage buys and
a love of colour have added depth to Janice Issitt's
1980s home in Buckinghamshire

FEATURE **KATIE HALLETT** PHOTOGRAPHS **RACHEL WHITING**

**ABOVE** Janice has painted one of the living room walls in Annie Sloan's vibrant 'Florence' paint **LEFT** The landing is painted in 'Barcelona Orange' by Annie Sloan and the cupboard is from Namaste. The clock belonged to Janice's dad and the other items were bought by him in Egypt **FAR LEFT** The Jesus statue in the guest bedroom was bought from a car boot sale **FACING PAGE, CLOCKWISE FROM TOP LEFT** The conservatory houses Janice's wool, vintage fabrics and sewing and knitting tools; 'My dresser is a homage to Sweden and displays my collection of antique Dala horses,' says Janice; the detail above the window in the dining hall is an old Indian carved door panel while the shutters are Georgian and were bought from a reclamation yard

*'With vintage items being so fashionable I have the opportunity to mix proper antiques with mid-century items. It's very restrictive sticking to one era especially if you love everything like I do!'*

Janice Issitt has loved antiques for as long as she can remember. Her dad collected and restored old clocks and when she was growing up she would spend many a Saturday visiting the V&A with him.

Her home – a detached 1980s property in a Buckinghamshire village – isn't what you'd expect of a typical antiques lover, though. Walls are painted in vibrant Indian-inspired hues; the only glass cabinet is in the kitchen; and, while the dining hall displays her collection of antique Swedish Dala horses, upstairs are groups of Egyptian perfume bottles and sumptuous gilt clocks. Her tastes are eclectic to say the least. 'With vintage items being so fashionable at the moment I have the opportunity to mix proper antiques with mid-century items that I remember from my childhood,' she says. 'It's very restrictive sticking to one era – especially if you love everything like I do!'

Janice moved here from London with her partner Ian five years ago and the couple's biggest challenge was making the 1980s house appear much older, as, although the Victorian-style exterior belied its age, the interior didn't. A period fireplace bought on eBay was fitted in the living room, the kitchen worktops and handles were replaced and the pine units painted, and the tiny bathroom extended to provide space for a slipper bath.

Their belongings provided depth, too. 'Before we moved here I inherited my dad's antiques collections, ranging from clocks to Egyptian perfume bottles, and displaying them was important to me,' says Janice. Now, they are proudly on show along with her own finds. Some of her thriftier buys include the now-white overmantel in the living room (£60 from an antiques centre) and the purple jug on the dining table (£5 from Tring Market Auctions).

Also showcased throughout her home is Janice's talent for making things. 'We were snowed in one Christmas so I decided to make the quilt that now hangs above our bed and I recently taught myself to knit Fair Isle socks by watching YouTube videos,' she says. Her home, too, could be described as something of a project and she admits that she's not ready to put away the paintbrushes just yet. 'I'll often wake up, inspired to repaint one of the walls,' she says. 'The office has changed colour five times in the last month!' ■

*Visit Janice's blog at janiceissittlifestyle.blogspot.com*

**ABOVE** The patchwork quilt above the bed was hand-stitched by Janice. 'The blankets and cushion are made from old Kantha saris,' says Janice. 'Mine are from The Bohemian Beach Company via eBay. Ziggy the cat was born in this very room!' **LEFT** A collection of clocks restored by Janice's dad in the master bedroom **FAR LEFT** Janice and Ian created a large bathroom by knocking through a wall into a small fourth bedroom. The lavabo (a contraption designed for hand washing) was bought from Heartfelt Designs

# Get the look
# VINTAGE

*Look for small details, unique furnishings and subtle hues
to get that sought-after distinguished look*

1 My Poppet Petite vintage patchwork cushion, £28, Not on the High Street 2 Sanderson squirrel and dove cushion, £50, John Lewis 3 Meakin coffee
pot, £32.90, China Search 4 Midnight cocktail shaker, £65, The Old Cinema 5 French table water bottle, £6.95, Dotcomgiftshop 6 Wire egg basket,
£19.50, Boutique Provencale 7 Wingback sofa, £325, Aspace 8 'Lazy Joe' chair, £338, Shackletons 9 SMEG fridge, £1,149, John Lewis 10 Sagaform cup
and saucer, £15, Cloudberry Living 11 Hand-woven geometric rug, £90, Oscar & Eve 12 'Windrush' dining table, £284, The Cotswold Company
13 'Loft' desk lamp, £155, Rose and Grey ✤ *For stockist information see page 130*

# Country chic

*From traditional farmhouse to contemporary cottage, these homes are full of rustic charm*

**KATIE HALLETT,**
HOMES EDITOR

**Aga? Check. Beamed** ceiling? Check. A dog bouncing at your heels? Check. These quintessentially English abodes will have you yearning to sling on your Hunters and move to the country. The proportions of the rooms and views from the luxuriously large windows are beguiling but the interiors themselves are also cause for celebration. A cosy, comforting feel is achieved with soothing wall colours that echo that of the surrounding countryside, blue and white antique china is displayed on open shelving (or even better, a dresser). And yes, there are plaids. This is the British country at its most stylish.

# Family heirlooms

*Diana and Tim Hare have achieved a grown-up yet relaxed feel in their Yorkshire farmhouse, which has been in Tim's family for over 70 years*

FEATURE **KATIE HALLETT** PHOTOGRAPHS **BEN ANDERS**

The kitchen is Diana's favourite room in the house – and where she spends most of her time. The huge farmhouse table was made by her uncle and the chairs are covered in a jolly tartan

*'We knew we wanted to make the kitchen bigger (it eventually quadrupled in size) but we spent a year planning and it took another year to be completed'*

**ABOVE** Black and white encaustic tiles have been teamed with Dulux's bright 'Early Bird' paint and traditional English antiques in the grand entrance hall
**LEFT** Light silk fabrics from James Hare add to the luxurious feel of the room
**FACING PAGE** The beamed drawing room has been decorated with Chinese lamp bases, oil paintings, a gilt mirror and plenty of silk. The sofa is from Multiyork

Listen to Diana Hare talk about her life in her North Yorkshire farmhouse and you can't help but dream about swapping city living for a more hearty, rural existence. 'Most family time is spent in the kitchen,' she says. 'When my husband Tim and I and our three children moved in, we knew we would need a kitchen that lived up to the rigours of life in the country: dogs, mud, people coming and going. This fits the bill and also has an Aga so it's continually toasty and there's always a dog lying on your feet.'

Located in the centre of a small hamlet, the building's impressive Georgian facade gives way to a home that is much smaller than you might imagine. It dates back to the Jacobean era and has been in the Hare family since the 1940s, when it served as the hamlet's farm, although then it looked rather different. The apple store was located in what is now Diana and Tim's bedroom; the coach house was incorporated into the now enviable kitchen; and the garden, well, that was mostly farmland. 'The farmer's wife loved gardening but her husband wasn't keen on giving up land used for crops so, when we moved in, we pretty much had a blank canvas,' says Diana.

The house, too, underwent a thorough transformation. 'We were lucky enough to keep on our tiny cottage, 12 miles away, while the work was being done here,' she explains. 'We knew we wanted to make the kitchen larger (it eventually quadrupled in size) but we spent a year planning and it took another year for everything to be completed – at one stage, the roof was off and the floorboards were out, so you could see right through to the cellar.'

During the planning stages, Diana experimented with different paint hues to find the right shades. 'It was so helpful having the time to decide. You soon realise that certain shades grow old quickly. I was determined not to go for beige but I can see why people do.' Instead, she opted for green walls with accents of lively patterns and softer silks (Tim is the managing director of the family business, silk company James Hare). However, she says that when they first moved in, the style was much more fussy: 'It's never been the sort of house that suited swags and tails but in our bedroom we did originally have a four-poster bed.' Finds from the family's trips overseas enhance the homely feel, although Diana laughs that they probably 'aren't quite suitable for a traditional farmhouse!' We beg to differ…

*To find out more about James Hare, visit james-hare.com*

'*It was so helpful having time to decide on paint hues. You soon realise that certain shades grow old quickly. I was determined not to go for beige but I can see why people do* '

**CLOCKWISE FROM TOP LEFT** 'I have about 40 or 50 hats, collected from trips around the world. I love their weird and wonderful shapes,' says Diana of the straw hats displayed around her home; Diana has arranged some of her hat collection in pretty labelled boxes above the wardrobes; a cushioned window seat adds comfort to the bathrrom; peonies from the garden brighten the entrance hall **FACING PAGE** This impressive master bedroom, with its vaulted, exposed-beamed ceiling, used to be the farm's apple store

**THIS PAGE** The kitchen had been modernised before the family moved in. The top half of the dresser, which displays Dawn's collection of blue and white china, was bought at the Bath Vintage & Antiques Market **FACING PAGE** Dawn and Will live on Marshfield Farm, which has become famous for its ice cream

# The sweet taste of success

*You might think that a 17th-century farmhouse overlooking the Cotswold hills sounds like the ultimate country dream, but for Dawn and Will Hawking it gets even better...*

FEATURE **KATIE HALLETT** PHOTOGRAPHS **JASON INGRAM**

*'The house has been in the family for generations. They had left their legacies and we wanted to leave ours'*

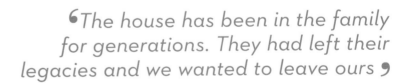

**CLOCKWISE FROM TOP LEFT** The floor in the kitchen is a honed and filled sandstone from Mandarin Stone; the mahogany coffee table in the 'yellow' living room is a family heirloom: 'It was a dining table but had a dodgy leg so we cut it down to make a coffee table,'; the bathroom has been one of the more recent renovations; Dawn and Will love India, which is reflected in the rich decor of the master bedroom; plants are arranged in a wire-framed display against the wall in the extended kitchen **FACING PAGE** The book shelves in the kitchen/dining extension are painted in Farrow & Ball's 'Teresa's Green'. The bamboo chairs belonged to Dawn's great uncle who was commodore of the Ben Line fleet, which travelled between Leith and Hong Kong in the 1950s and 1960s

It's hard to imagine a dreamier lifestyle than that of the Hawking family. Not only do they live in a smart but welcoming 17th-century farmhouse with views that stretch to the Cotswold hills, it's located just a few steps from their family-run business: Marshfield Farm Ice Cream. The commute is a breeze and the house is temptingly close to the ice-cream parlour where the family serve their delights to customers at weekends. Not surprisingly, Dawn Hawking admits that the family eat ice cream every day.

Will started the business with his father 25 years ago and Dawn became involved in 1991. But it wasn't until 10 years ago that the couple and their three children – Flora, Angus and Rory – moved to the farmhouse. 'We were living in a cottage down the road but decided to swap with Will's parents, who had lived in the farmhouse since the 1970s,' says Dawn. 'We were delighted – it was great to have all the extra space for the children, plus living next to the farm with its 250 cows made things so much easier.'

Luckily, Will's parents had done plenty of work on the farmhouse before Dawn and Will moved here – uncovering fireplaces behind brick walls, reconfiguring rooms and the garden – so most of the changes the couple made were purely cosmetic. The main transformation, and where Will and Dawn wanted to make their mark, was in the kitchen. 'The house has been in the family for generations, and we wanted to leave our legacy,' says Dawn.

What was once a relatively small, dark space has been transformed with a large extension into a light, bright living area that is now clearly the hub of the home. Natural stone flooring was introduced, along with beautiful botanical wallpaper and a reconditioned 1940s Aga, which, says Dawn, the room was 'crying out for'. Windows now line the width of the dining area, which overlooks the beautiful garden. 'It's been lovely to expose the view and the extra space makes it fantastic for entertaining,' says Dawn. 'In fact, it was finished just in time to host an Olympic Games opening ceremony party.'

The kitchen is also where Dawn displays two of her passions: blue and white china, and jugs. 'I inherited my mother's habit for blue and white,' she laughs. 'Some pieces used to belong to her, some I've bought from the Bath Vintage & Antiques Market and a couple were actually given to me by a lady who attended one of our farm tours.' As for the jugs, they're picked up from 'all over the place'. 'I've collected them ever since I've had my own home – I wouldn't like to say how many I now own.'

It almost goes without saying that the children are pretty pleased to live on an ice-cream farm. 'Rory loves farming, Flo loves walking in the countryside and Angus loves hosting parties in the barn,' says Dawn. 'Naturally we're always inundated with their friends popping over for ice cream, too…' ∎
*To find out more about Marshfield Ice Cream visit marshfield-icecream.co.uk*

# Love at first sight

*In 2000, Helen and Alasdair Scott fell in love with the Cornish village of Mousehole, where they later decided to set about restoring a 19th-century cottage*

FEATURE **KATHERINE SORRELL** PHOTOGRAPHS **IAIN KEMP**

**TOP LEFT** Helen and Alasdair in the kitchen of their Cornish cottage **THIS PAGE** Alasdair made the planked dining table using old pine and the chairs were picked up at a French *brocante*

**TOP** A white loose cover ensures that the sofa – an Ikea piece bought on eBay – looks pristine. Helen has piled embroidered cushions and a quilt, all from the local Sandpiper Gallery, on to it for added comfort **ABOVE** Alasdair has built small storage cupboards into the space below the stairs **LEFT** Painted in Farrow & Ball's 'Smoked Trout', the living room is airy and welcoming **FACING PAGE, CLOCKWISE FROM TOP LEFT** Helen made the pretty roll-up blind in the bathroom using fabric from Cath Kidston; a gorgeous French Rococo bed makes a focal point for the master bedroom; the bathroom echoes the coastal location of the cottage

*'If you buy new, you've instantly lost money, but if you buy antiques or collectables wisely, you can make your money back. It's also the ultimate form of recycling!'*

Helen and her husband Alasdair bought this Cornish cottage after falling in love with Mousehole while on holiday. 'As soon as we drove into the village on New Year's Day 2000 we were hooked,' explains Helen. 'This place has some sort of magic that entraps you. Alasdair had always wanted to live by the sea and we were outgrowing our maisonette in Leamington Spa, so it made sense to relocate.'

As Alasdair is a self-employed builder they had the freedom to act on what most people merely daydream about and, less than a year later, the couple and their son Josh were heading west. Helen initially went to see Gone Fishing Cottage on behalf of her parents, who were also thinking of relocating. An end-of-terrace granite house with a slate roof, it was built around 1875 on three storeys. It looked somewhat warehouse-like and inside there was Eighties-style textured plasterwork throughout and signs of damp. 'Alasdair and I hadn't originally considered the cottage because it was slightly out of budget and looked so ugly from the outside,' says Helen. 'But as soon as I saw inside I was blown away. It wasn't right for my parents but I could see its potential for us.'

The couple made an offer immediately and, after moving in, started work on the renovation. 'One of the first things I did was to chip the white paint off the side of the house,' explains Alasdair, who used to work as an antiques dealer and is now a carpenter and builder. 'It would originally have been lime-washed but modern paint had sealed in the damp, so once that came off it made a huge difference.' Alasdair has always endeavoured to retain as many original features as possible, including doors, wall panelling and timber. He also made a number of pieces from scratch, including the tongue-and-groove kitchen cupboards, the impressive 'dresser' in the dining area (actually a cover for a storage heater), the dining table and the cupboards that neatly fit the spaces above the stairs.

Almost all the other furnishings in the cottage are antique or vintage, 'My mother used to own an antiques centre so I grew up going to auctions with her – everything in our house came from a sale,' says Alasdair. 'If you buy new you've instantly lost money but if you buy antiques or collectables wisely, you can make your money back. It's also the ultimate form of recycling!' ∎

*For more information on Gone Fishing Cottage B&B visit gonefishingcottage.co.uk*

# Modern makeover

*Digging into the basement, extending up into the roof and doing an eco-makeover has given this 1960s bungalow in Suffolk a new lease of life*

FEATURE **ANGELA LINFORTH** PHOTOGRAPHS **RACHEL WHITING**

**CLOCKWISE FROM TOP LEFT** The table on the deck was made by Fay Sweet's builder using scaffolding boards and table legs from Ikea; Fay can now paint all year round; vintage Poole Pottery designed in the 1950s and 1960s; the dining room is open-plan to the sitting room. It used to contain two bedrooms and a bathroom. The vintage wing chair has been covered in John Lewis fabric; the dining table is an antique find that was reconditioned. It sits below a Poulsen lamp **FACING PAGE** Fay updated the kitchen by spraying the units orange

*'It presented itself as the ultimate project, sitting alone in the countryside with far-reaching views over pasture and woods'*

It's not unusual to find the odd surprise when you move into your new home but, when artist Fay Sweet took the keys for her Suffolk bungalow, she was taken aback to discover a mysterious secret house in a barn in the grounds. 'I'd been to look around on a few occasions but the barn had been locked every time. It was only when I moved in and could get into the barn that I realised it contained a whole mini-house. It was even hooked up to Sky TV!'

Strange buildings aside (and the rumours locally about its use were colourful), the bungalow presented itself as the ultimate project, sitting in the countryside near Halesworth with far-reaching views over pasture and woods. A veteran of three previous renovations, Fay felt that this place showed a lot of promise. 'I had often walked past it and thought it would never come up for sale. Then, suddenly, it came on the market. I thought there was so much potential to bring the light in and make it idyllic.'

Fay had worked with the architect she eventually chose, Robert Gooderham, before and once finally underway, the construction was relatively smooth. It took about a year and involved building into the roof, opening up the interior and installing huge floor-to-ceiling windows. Part of the plan also involved making the building super eco-efficient: insulation was layered on to the building, and heating and hot water are now via a ground source heat pump and a few trusty wood burners.

As far as possible, materials were recycled, including the old kitchen, which was sprayed orange and rearranged. Fay used a mix of handmade pieces (a four-poster bed in the main bedroom and a garden table), finds from Islington's Criterion auction rooms, plus assorted junk-shop buys.

And the mysterious secret house? It's now gone forever – but not before being immortalised in a friend's crime novel. ■

*To see Fay's paintings, visit faysweet.com*

# A countryside proposal

*When Sarah Woods stumbled across this house in the Yorkshire Dales, she knew it was perfect, although owning it came as a total surprise...*

FEATURE **KATIE HALLETT** PHOTOGRAPHS **BEN ANDERS**

**CLOCKWISE FROM TOP LEFT** The framed train cigarette cards in the downstairs hall belonged to Nich's father and Sarah reframed them as a birthday gift; the French bed and bedside table were both bought during a buying trip in Paris; the tiny silver jewellery box was a gift from Sarah's uncle on her 21st birthday. The larger box was given to her by her father; Sarah was given these old books by Nich's grandmother; tartan fabric, antique chair and oversized lantern add interest to the upstairs landing **FACING PAGE** 'The antique silver bowl was a wedding gift from one of my closest friends,' says Sarah

*'Tucked away in a tiny North Yorkshire village, it offered bags of potential to become a cosy little country retreat. The couple were just bowled over'*

# Antique celebration

*A 17th-century house in picturesque Buckinghamshire has proved to be the perfect family home for antiques lover Caroline Johnston*

FEATURE **KATIE HALLETT** PHOTOGRAPHS **MARK BOLTON**

**LEFT** Homeowner Caroline Johnston in her 1960s MGA **THIS PAGE** The freestanding kitchen is from Fired Earth and the room is filled with antiques, such as an early 20th-century brass cork screw; a collection of original 'Italian' by Spode is displayed in a 19th-century plate rack

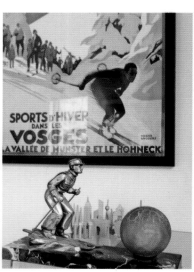

**CLOCKWISE FROM TOP** The couple's French dining table sits in the impressive garden extension; a reproduction 1920s skiing poster hangs above an original art deco skier lamp; the rocking chair to the left of the fireplace in the living room dates from the mid-19th century, the child's rocking chair from 1820; a pine crockery shelf has been dressed with Laura Ashley fabric

The mid-18th century long case clock in the living room is from Worboys Antiques. The sofa is one of the few modern pieces in the house and is from Sofa Workshop

Tucked away in the south Buckinghamshire countryside with a large pond between the garden and meadow, Caroline Johnston's home couldn't be in a more idyllic setting. However, although the storybook location was obviously a draw, it was the unusual shape and history of the 17th-century house that won her and husband Nigel over.

'The children, Jonathan, Cameron and Frazer, love the individuality of the place, too – and when they were younger, the pond was often the site of raft building and plank walking,' says Caroline.

Caroline and Nigel are both keen antiques lovers and saw the house as the perfect backdrop for their collections, although when they first moved in this wasn't quite the case. 'The house had been renovated and modernised a decade before we bought it but the lovely original features looked lost in the contemporary setting,' explains Caroline. 'We wanted to make it more genuine and so ripped out anything deemed too modern, swapping the plastic light switches for Jim Lawrence beeswax finish dolly switches and replacing the carpets with wooden flooring from the West Sussex Timber Company.' Along with the smaller touches, the couple refitted the bathrooms, added a garden room – a wooden framed glass extension that now houses a 14ft 19th-century dining table – and, most spectacularly, a swimming pool. To avoid the pool looking too incongruous against its surroundings, the couple opted for a darker, more natural shade, rather than the conventional Mediterranean blue. 'We didn't want it to jar with the scenery, so kept it all very natural,' says Caroline.

Now, the garden is one of the family's favourite places to relax and even when they're not outside, they can still enjoy it from the house. 'The windows all look out onto different aspects of the garden and countryside, which is very tranquil. I love how there's a beautiful view from every window.'

In terms of the interior, the couple have kept the walls light with muted shades, which enhance the appearance of the wooden beams and are the perfect foil to their carefully selected antique furniture. The couple have made a conscious effort to fill the house with pieces from the 17th century (when the property was built) onwards, with items sourced from a wide range of locations. 'We bought the 19th-century dining table over a decade ago from France,' explains Caroline. 'The antiques business was less internet-based then so when we saw an advert in a magazine for a dealer in Rouen, we drove all the way over there to buy it – and then drove straight back again!'

Although the house is bursting with antique pieces, Caroline is careful not to be too precious with them. 'I love filling our home with pieces that have a history but we try to use as much in day-to-day life as possible – they're meant to be enjoyed.' Along with the table and other furniture, Caroline counts antique wine glasses, items from the suffragette movement and the paintings among her best-loved items in the house. 'Although not strictly in the home, the classic cars are great fun,' she confesses. 'We've collected them for 25 years and now have three. The MGA is a more recent addition and it's my favourite. Perfect for country jaunts.'

people

se of

the log

te.com

*'I love filling our home with pieces that have a history but we try to use as much in day-to-day life as possible – they're meant to be enjoyed '*

**TOP** Caroline bought the bed from Laura Ashley and has combined Laura Ashley bed linen with a French antique fabric cushion **LEFT** The heart-shaped wreath on the bathroom door is from Not on the High Street **FAR LEFT** The bathroom fittings and green tiles are from Fired Earth

# Get the look
# COUNTRY

*Whether you're after an armchair, a candlestick or a decorative hen, these rustic accessories will give your home an authentic country look*

*Stylist's* PICK

**1** 19th century mahogany clock, £2,200, The Old Cinema **2** Jug, £29.95, Emma Bridgewater **3** Toast rack, £12.50, Paperchase **4** Paul Costelloe Living Albany cabinet, £935, Dunnes Stores **5** 'Queen Anne' wing chair, £2,115, Wesley Barrell **6** 'Mensa' candlestick, £57.41, Papa Theo **7** bronze plant theatre, £49.95, Not on the High Street **8** 'Jules' quilt, £75, Feather and Black **9** Polka dot hen, £49.95, Emma Bridgewater **10** 'Richardson' three-seater sofa, from £2,000, Sofa Workshop **11** Baroque photo frame, £8, Wilkinson **12** Treasure chest, £79, Eastern Influence ❖ *For stockist information see page 130*

# French decorative

*A keen eye for detail (and the occasional trip over the Channel) gave these homes their super-chic look*

**KATIE HALLETT**,
HOMES EDITOR

**Ah, the French.** They're a stylish lot. Although famed for their elegant sartorial style, their interiors are equally as inspiring. Often typified by ornate chandeliers dripping with glass, elaborately carved bedframes and distressed white-painted furniture, French decorative is all about faded grandeur. These homeowners have trawled French *brocantes* and English flea markets and managed to create what sounds like the impossible – a relaxed, effortless look that's at the same time glamorous. The muted paint colours play an important part in the scheme too and help amplify light, especially when teamed with plenty of foxed mirrors (à la Karen Cull's Cotswold cottage).

# Cultured influences

*Soothing paint colours and French-inspired furnishings create an elegant feel in interior designer Abbie de Bunsen's Victorian terrace*

FEATURE **KATIE HALLETT** PHOTOGRAPHS **RACHEL WHITING**

**LEFT** Collections of glass have been grouped together on the distressed dining room sideboard. The painting was bought at Portobello Market **THIS PAGE** The drawing room is homeowner Abbie's favourite room in the house. The cushions are from Chelsea Textiles and Bennison and the velvet sofa is upholstered in an Andrew Martin fabric. The cream woven curtains are from Malabar

*'I absolutely love French furniture and antiques. Many holidays have been spent in Paris, rootling around brocantes and discovering out-of-the-way markets'*

**CLOCKWISE FROM TOP LEFT** Abbie loves the painting by Tor Falcon in the dining room; the drawing room has been painted using SC264 by Papers and Paints; the dresser in the kitchen is filled with Emma Bridgewater pottery; the table and benches in the breakfast room have been painted and antiqued by Abbie; the kitchen looks through to the playroom. White letters can be found in John Lewis

The beautiful French bed and wardrobe in the master bedroom are from Mark Maynard in Tunbridge Wells

'When friends first visited our new home they joked that they couldn't tell we'd moved,' recalls interior designer Abbie de Bunsen. 'My husband James and I love Victorian architecture, with its generous ceiling height and cornicing. But Victorian terraces in London do tend to have identical layouts so, when we moved out of a terrace in Clapham to one in Wandsworth, we knew we would have to work on the decor to create a different feel.'

Despite the fact that Abbie's job entails designing different looks in her clients' homes, she cites deciding on how to decorate her own house as one of the biggest challenges she faced when she and James moved over a decade ago. 'We were lucky in that we only had to make cosmetic changes. My biggest problem was committing to a scheme and sticking to it,' she says. 'I can torture myself for months about colours.' The current light-filled interior certainly belies the hours spent deliberating over paint colours, flooring options and woodwork finishes. The kitchen is now a crisp, soothing shade of green, kept light with whitewashed furniture and a limestone floor, while in the drawing room, seagrass flooring has been fitted and walls are painted in a restful duck egg blue. Tactile, cosseting fabrics and touches of silver and glass complete the look. 'It's so important for rooms to calm and inspire us. The large bay windows help, of course – the Victorians definitely knew what they were doing.'

It's impossible not to notice a French influence when walking through the terrace, which is also home to the couple's children, Violet and Hugo. Downstairs, red ginghams adorn chair cushions; upstairs, a white-painted French bed and dainty chandelier add a distinctively Gallic feel in the master bedroom. 'I lived in Paris in my late teens and love French furniture and antiques,' explains Abbie. 'I've spent many holidays over there since, rootling around *brocantes*. There's probably at least one thing in each room that reminds me of a different trip.'

Abbie admits that the constant temptation to buy for her own home comes with the territory of being an interior designer but she's been careful to edit her belongings down, combining French finds with paintings picked up from Portobello Road, antique mahogany furniture and contemporary soft furnishings. 'Growing up, I'd spend a lot of time trawling through antiques shops with my mother – that love of old furniture has just stuck.' ■

*For more information on Abbie de Bunsen Design, visit abbiedebunsen.com*

# A touch of elegance

*Karen Price has transformed a 17th-century property from a tired bakery into a stylish B&B with more than a hint of the Provençal about it...*

FEATURE **KATIE HALLETT** PHOTOGRAPHS **JASON INGRAM**

**CLOCKWISE FROM TOP LEFT** Karen originally wanted a completely free-standing kitchen but realised she needed work surfaces, too. She compromised by having units made by a local carpenter and fitting open shelving to the walls; in the summer the second courtyard area is something of a suntrap; the living room was formerly the village post office and when Karen arrived the room still contained the original counters and desks. The fireplace had been boarded up and the original bread oven was hidden beneath the cladding **FACING PAGE** Karen relaxes in the front garden – which was previously a driveway – with her Jack Russell, Monty

Karen Price makes it all look very easy. Her country home – in the blink-and-you'll-miss-it village of Chewton Mendip near Wells – looks like it would be more at home in Provence: all flagstone floors, iridescent lime-rendered walls and elegant antique furnishings. Appearances can be deceptive though and the polished finish belies a year of hard grafting.

When Karen bought the 17th-century house seven years ago she was after a renovation project and this place couldn't have been more of one. What is now the sitting room was the village post office; the dining room was originally a bakery; and the kitchen, literally, a pig sty. 'During the viewing there was a whole pig being roasted in what was the bakery – which was filled with huge ovens – and the windows had fallen out on to the pavement. The property had been in the previous owners' family for around 90 years and it was falling down around their ears,' says Karen. This is the fourth historic building Karen's worked on, so it was in very safe hands. She enlisted the help of a local builder who was 'very sympathetic to the house's history' and together they oversaw the work of the plumber, electrician and lime plasterer. 'Through experience I've learnt the importance of getting the walls right,' she says. The previous owners had covered walls in painted woodchip and, when the builder started to remove it, the plaster just fell away in chunks. As a result the walls were taken back to their barest form and painted in the traditional lime plaster. The method produces a lovely chalky

finish but, more importantly, it lets walls breathe – preventing any future damp problems from developing.

Other major tasks included creating a kitchen from scratch from what was previously the pig sty and garage, and turning a driveway into a pretty front courtyard. The kitchen units were made by a local carpenter and open shelves give the room a relaxed feel. The kitchen and courtyard are now connected by French doors and are one of Karen's favourite features of the renovated home. 'In the summer months, when the doors are flung open, it feels like one space. When it's warm enough, I love serving breakfast out there.'

The feat of converting a predominantly commercial space into a home would be enough to fill most with dread and, although Karen admits to having experienced many a sleepless night, she says that embracing the experience is the best, and indeed the only, option: 'You soon realise that there's no going back. You have to be brave and enjoy it rather than letting it scare you.'

Karen's father was an interior designer and, once the structural work was complete, her inherited design instinct kicked in and she set about filling the interior with French finds and gorgeous pieces bought from local antiques fairs. 'I grew up visiting France so have always been inspired by the French look,' she says. 'But recently I've become more country than decorative: opting for as free-standing a kitchen as possible and a painted courtyard covered with wall-climbing vines.' ∎

*For details of staying at Karen's home, visit theposthousebandb.com*

*'You soon realise there's no going back. You have to be brave and enjoy it rather than letting it scare you '*

**ABOVE** Ticking fabrics and a headboard created from an old wooden panel ensure a rustic feel in the bedroom **LEFT** Blooms from the garden bring the outside in **FAR LEFT** The bathroom is furnished with a washstand found in a Wells antiques shop and roll-top bath **FACING PAGE, CLOCKWISE FROM LEFT** The couple bought the imposing fireplace from a reclamation yard in Bristol and the French refectory table from a dealer in Wells; the dining room was formerly a bakery and, when Karen moved in, a quarter of the room was filled with old ovens; weck jars and bottles display jams and roses

# Starting from scratch

*After eight years in Mallorca, Anthony and Karen Cull had to rebuild their antiques collection for their very English cottage in the Cotswolds*

FEATURE **ROSANNA MORRIS** PHOTOGRAPHS **JASON INGRAM**

**THIS PAGE** A neutral colour scheme and sisal flooring keep the cottage bright. The Flamant linen sofa is from Obi & Moo in Bath **FACING PAGE** Homeowner Karen Cull and her dog Molly at the front door

When Karen and Anthony Cull decided to return to Gloucestershire after living in Mallorca for eight years, it wasn't just a new house they had to find. They had to gather new furniture, new artwork and new ornaments – the whole kit and caboodle. Because, no sooner had they put their spacious converted flour mill on the market, they found a buyer who not only wanted the house but its entire contents as well.

In the UK, Karen and Anthony were looking for something completely different to their Spanish home and they found it – in the form of a two-bedroom 16th-century thatched cottage in the Cotswold village of Gretton. 'We were leaving something really special behind so we wanted something special to move into,' says Karen. 'We felt it was right as soon as we stepped inside. Although it needed updating we knew we could adapt it.'

It was black and white inside and out – 'All the beams and doors, even the walk-in wardrobes, were black!' she says. The couple set about lightening up the interior using a palette of off-white paints and soft furnishings. In the compact galley kitchen they had beautiful oak cabinets handmade by Abbey Kitchens and

removed light-consuming built-in cupboards from the rest of the interior. The most recent change though is the bathroom, which has a new bateau bath and a porcelain sink. 'It was all looking a bit smart for us so we toned it down by creating a cupboard door from an old French shutter,' says Karen.

Elsewhere, the mix-and-match approach continues. A gym bench-cum-coffee table sits comfortably with balustrade lamps in the living room, while chandeliers and painted furniture add verve to the bedrooms and dining room.

Karen's new life as an antiques dealer (she has a shop in Winchcombe), has helped her to furnish the house in just a few years, while making it look like a lifetime of collecting. The only difficulty is deciding what to sell and what to keep. 'When we left Spain, we had to part with some fabulous pieces,' says Karen. 'It worked out well, though, as they probably wouldn't have fitted in here. It enabled us to start again and hand pick pieces as we found them, which was fun.' The couple started with the bare essentials: the bed and the sofa. But Karen admits that they've now changed everything about two or three times. She has found some keepers, too. 'The wooden horses and Provençal pottery will stay with us forever.'
*For more on Anton & K Decorative Antiques and Interiors, visit antonandk.co.uk*

*'We felt it was right as soon as we stepped inside. Although it needed updating, we knew we could adapt it'*

**CLOCKWISE FROM TOP LEFT** The French bed, complemented by the French chandelier in the high-ceilinged spare room; to keep the compact kitchen light and airy, Karen had the oak worktops bleached; the French button-back chair and bespoke lamp in the spare room are from Anton & K; Karen and Anthony toned down the bathroom with French finds – a 'coiffure' sign and an old painted shutter
**FACING PAGE** Painted furniture and pottery complete the air of faded grandeur

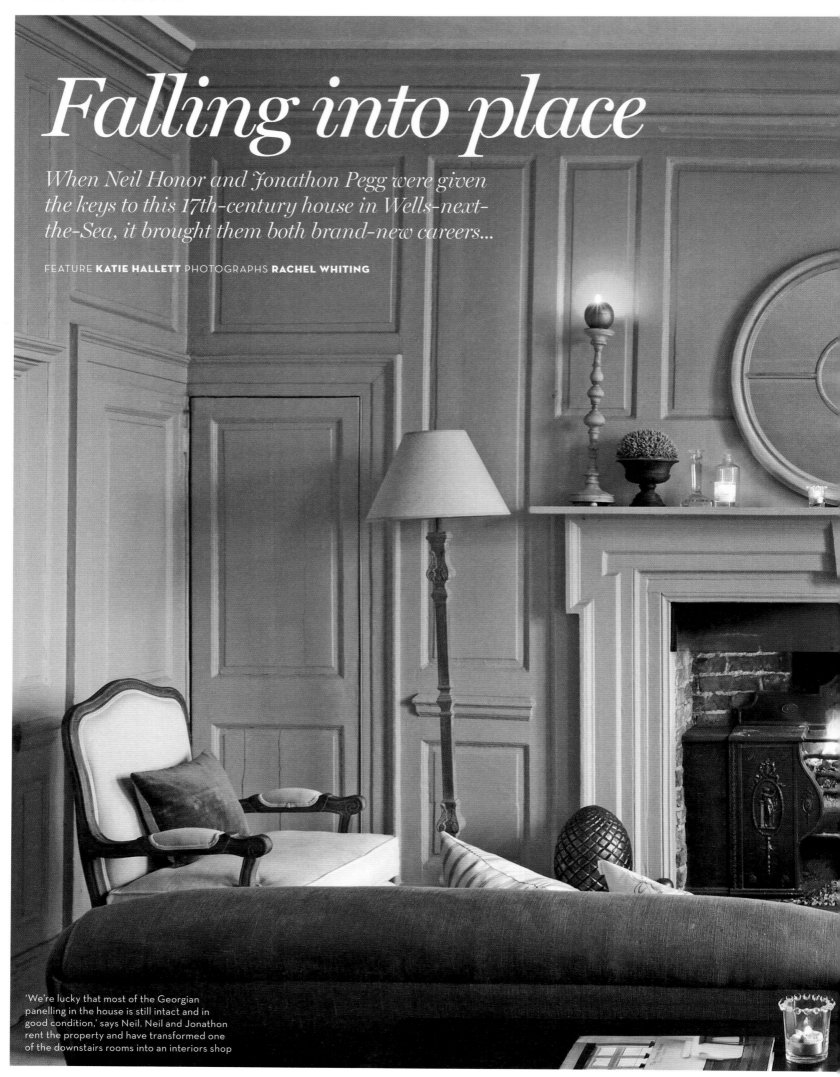

# Falling into place

*When Neil Honor and Jonathon Pegg were given the keys to this 17th-century house in Wells-next-the-Sea, it brought them both brand-new careers...*

FEATURE **KATIE HALLETT** PHOTOGRAPHS **RACHEL WHITING**

'We're lucky that most of the Georgian panelling in the house is still intact and in good condition,' says Neil. Neil and Jonathon rent the property and have transformed one of the downstairs rooms into an interiors shop

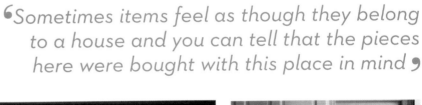

'Sometimes items feel as though they belong to a house and you can tell that the pieces here were bought with this place in mind '

**CLOCKWISE FROM TOP LEFT** Neil says 'the wall mirror was a fully glazed window before we got it cut into its curvy shape'; the kitchen was built by a local carpenter before the couple moved in; Neil (left) and Jonathon (right) in their living room; 'the key to decorating a black-painted bedroom is to use it as a backdrop for furnishings; 'we love traditional rush matting but this natural rug from Ikea was a fraction of the price,' says Neil

Sometimes things happen that are just so wonderfully serendipitous it's as if they're meant to be. Take this 17th-century former merchant's house in Wells-next-the-Sea in Norfolk. Its owner was moving to a house nearby but, as she was so attached to the property, didn't want to sell yet dreamt of it being turned into a business. Then she was introduced by a mutual friend to Neil Honor and Jonathon Pegg. Neil had just finished working for a PR company, had always wanted to open his own interiors shop and both he and Jonathon were itching to move from London. Just a month later, Neil and Jonathon had the keys. Three months after that, they had opened an interiors shop in a room of the house and, six months later, a concession in Warings Furniture in Norfolk opened. 'We came into each other's lives at the right time,' says Neil. 'Everything happened so quickly – we never questioned that it was where we were meant to be.'

What's even more remarkable is that the house was already decorated in a style that was very much what Neil and Jonathon's design ethos is all about: muted colours and classic pieces. It was love at first sight. 'Walking into the house felt like going back in time,' says Neil. 'It was a moonlit night and, inside, the crackling fire bathed the living room in a warm glow. Although the ceilings are high, the original panelling makes it cosy and it seemed like home immediately – we knew we had to live here.'

The idea for the shop, Catesby's, was conceived on their first viewing of the house. They had pulled back a heavy net curtain in the store room and noted that it looks out on to Wells's high street. 'Like a lot of people who work in desk-bound jobs in the city, I would daydream about starting my own business in a rural area – be it a cafe, florist or an interiors shop,' says Neil. 'As it happens, I ended up doing two-and-a-half of those things here: in the summer we run a tea garden from the courtyard and sell plants.' On moving in, the priority was getting Catesby's up and running and Neil gave himself the tight deadline of his birthday, a few weeks later, for the grand opening. 'Although the rest of the house was in great condition, we had to start from scratch with the shop: painting dark, dusty panelling, fitting electrics and reviving the original floorboards,' he says.

While the main elements of the living space have been left untouched, Neil and Jonathon have made the interior their own with soft furnishings and quirky – but still classic – accessories. Beautiful pieces, such as the mahogany cabinet in the living room and both of the beds, were already here. 'Sometimes items feel as though they belong to a house and you can tell that the pieces here were bought with this place in mind,' says Neil. In the living room the couple added the sea grass rugs to protect the sumptuous but not so practical cream carpet. In the black guest bedroom, golden blinds were made to inject some colour and, in the master bedroom, a mirror that belonged to a Victorian sideboard has been adapted as a headboard. 'The bare bones of the house were already here,' says Neil. 'Now it's mainly about maintaining it and adding layers of our own personal taste to the already elegant backdrop.' ■

*For more information on Catesby's, visit catesbys.co.uk*

# A *change* of scenery

*Izzy and Harry Judd have brought a cosy, country feel to this former artist's studio in Chiswick*

FEATURE **KATIE HALLETT** PHOTOGRAPHS **JO HENDERSON**

The painting in the living area was a wedding gift from Izzy's husband Harry's grandmother. 'It took Harry and I a while to agree on a painting we both liked but we both loved this,' says Izzy. 'It's by the Rocks Brothers who are twins and paint together.' The parquet floor was sanded and restored by Southern Cross Flooring and the spotlight is from an antiques fair in Hertfordshire

*'When you've spent time away from home, you realise there's nothing like your own bed and being surrounded by all your belongings'*

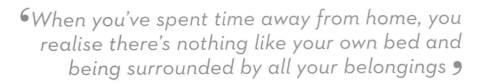

**CLOCKWISE FROM TOP LEFT** Izzy found the desk on eBay and the lamp was £20 from Sunbury Antiques Market; the dining section is open-plan to the living area. The dining table and benches are from the Sunbury Antiques Market and the Swedish clock is from Nordic Style. Izzy's Attic stocks similar distressed picture frames; the bathroom is one of the few closed-off areas of the house; the bedroom sits above the living area in the eaves of the building; 'The Cath Kidston Roberts radio was a Christmas gift from my mum and dad when I was 16 and away at school. I always have my radio on and I'm usually listening to Magic FM,' says Izzy **FACING PAGE** Morris the cat lounges in the master bedroom. The bed is from Feather & Black and the chest of drawers from Loaf

In 2011 Izzy Judd made a rather dramatic career change. She had spent her early twenties performing in electric string quartet Escala but, following a life-long passion for interiors, decided to switch arenas and TV studios for vintage markets and a desk firmly rooted at home.

Izzy had been toying with the idea of starting her own interiors business for years and, after buying her first home with husband Harry, the drummer from McFly, she decided to make the leap and launch online shop Izzy's Attic. The store combines one-off vintage finds with upcycled and handmade pieces and the same casual country aesthetic can be found in her home, which Izzy says they were 'so lucky' to find. 'We only gave ourselves one day to view places together as Harry was going to South America on tour the following day,' she says. 'We were shown about four properties in a row and I was beginning to get a bit downhearted as none of them felt right – but then we came here.'

'Here' is a 1930s former artist's studio in Chiswick. With its mezzanine bedroom and double-height ceiling, it's not the type of property to come up for sale very often. 'As we walked through the gate that leads to the row of four studios and into the garden, the smell of roses hit me – it felt like a secret garden,' says Izzy. The couple moved in during October 2011 and although they didn't want to make any structural changes, they had a list of smaller jobs to do. They stripped out carpets to reveal beautiful original parquet flooring,

which they had sanded, repainted the walls, removed shelves that divided the living and dining areas, and retiled the bathroom and en suite.

'It's quite a tricky layout as, aside from the bathrooms and spare bedroom, it's completely open-plan with our bedroom overlooking the living room. We had to think very carefully about how it could work,' says Izzy. The whole space needed to be painted in the same colour so there was added pressure to choose the right shade (Farrow & Ball's 'Borrowed Light') and everything had to be very cohesive.

Aside from a Brit award (discreetly tucked away on a sideboard) and framed McFly records, there's a distinct lack of showbiz in the home, which Izzy describes as 'a little bit French rustic, a little bit country farmhouse'. To create a cosy feel she scoured antiques fairs and shops for quirky pieces. 'I love finding something old and tired and seeing it transformed by a fresh setting.'

Despite being just a 10-minute walk from the underground, it's easy to forget that the studio is in the city. 'I love the peace that I feel when I'm here. It overlooks St Peter's Square garden and, being tucked away, it's really quiet,' says Izzy. 'When you've spent a lot of time away from home you realise that there's nothing like your own bed and being surrounded by all your belongings,' she says. ▪

*For more information on Izzy's online shop, visit izzysattic.co.uk*

# Simply stylish

*Sheila New has brought her keen eye for antiques to her 19th renovation project*
*– an early 20th-century property in the coastal town of Sidmouth*

FEATURE **KATIE HALLETT** PHOTOGRAPHS **RACHEL WHITING**

**CLOCKWISE FROM TOP LEFT** Sheila New outside her Sidmouth home; the vintage enamel coffee pots were picked up in market in Lille; Sheila believes flowers are essential to making a house a home; 'I love the look of white paint next to marble,' says Sheila; 'After seeing Monet's kitchen in Giverny, which had the most amazing blue and white tiles, I hunted for similar designs for years,' says Sheila **FACING PAGE** Sheila bought the French dining chairs at Ardingly Antique & Collectors Fair, while the pink cake stands are from RE

# FRENCH DECORATIVE

**THIS PAGE** The bureau in the living room is one of Sheila's favourite pieces **FACING PAGE, TOP** Sheila bought the porter's chair from a car boot sale and the rug from a second-hand shop for just £4 **FACING PAGE, BOTTOM** Sheila made this bed canopy by hanging antique drapes from a canopy found at an antiques fair. 'Antique canopies are often sold by French dealers at big fairs, such as Ardingly or Newark,' she says

*'I've spent my life in antiques fairs, traipsing around in the rain and the mud looking for lovely things '*

'I missed one out,' remembers Sheila New, when asked to count the number of homes that she's owned. 'There was also the thatched cottage that I bought on a whim when I went out to buy some spoons!' Sheila's current home – an early 20th-century house in the coastal town of Sidmouth in Devon – is her 19th address. And although Sheila completely gutted the place – ripping out laminate flooring, repainting colourful walls, removing marble fireplaces and replacing the built-in kitchen – she describes the year-long process as a 'doddle'. 'I once moved into a large Georgian house that was missing a floor. You could see right through to the cellar,' she says. 'And there was the place where my former husband and I had to remove the lower walls because the footing wasn't secure. That was pretty harrowing – I was bringing up five children at the time. So, although here I had to spend months hopping to a tiny spot in the living room that was only big enough for one chair while the rest of my furniture was piled against the wall, this project didn't faze me.'

It wasn't the condition of the house that brought Sheila here, though. In fact, she would much rather have sunk her teeth into a bigger challenge. But, after visiting Sidmouth with her daughter, she fell in love with the coastline and, coincidentally, had just put property number 18 on to the market. She confesses that, yes, she's something of a 'serial renovator'. In fact, she tackled her first project – a derelict Victorian terrace – when she was only 18.

As well as only buying properties that she can improve, Sheila finds it hard to think of a piece of furniture or decoration of hers that's brand new or that hasn't been revamped. 'If it's lovely and rotten, that's the piece I want. I bring it home and hope for the best,' she says. Hence the kitchen table she bought for £3 from a local recycling centre and sanded and repainted, the ornate bed canopies from various antiques fairs and the fireplace in the living room – a lucky salvage find – cut to size by a builder. 'I've spent my life in antiques fairs, traipsing around in the rain and the mud looking for lovely things,' she says. 'My dad would take me to Rag Alley – a market on Westmoreland Road in Southwark, London – when I was growing up and we would buy all sorts of rubbish. Now I've just moved on to better rags.'

She's being modest. Far from rags, Sheila's home is full of beautifully aged pieces of furniture, rich fabrics and pretty accessories which, when combined, create an overall feel of romance, something she refers to as 'dishevelled elegance'. It may all appear effortless but, in order to tie the look together, Sheila has a few 'rules'. No curtains in small rooms as 'it interrupts the line of the window'. Nothing should have a barcode. A little bit of red goes a long way. And, if there's anything that you aren't sure about, remove it. But most simply, when it comes to interiors, Sheila believes in 'flowers, books, a few pictures, plain walls and floors – and Radio 4.' ∎

# New beginnings

*When Keith and Maggie Beasley retired, they decided not to put their feet up, but to transform a shabby 19th-century cottage into something rather beautiful*

FEATURE **KATIE HALLETT** PHOTOGRAPHS **RACHEL WHITING**

**ABOVE LEFT** 'We love the spacious entrance hall with its exposed stone bricks and galleried landing,' says Maggie. 'It feels very light for a cottage.' **ABOVE RIGHT** The open-plan dining area is decorated in neutral shades. The pictures were collected on the couple's travels **BELOW** The wood-burning stove was already in situ when the couple moved here and Maggie loves the warmth it brings to the living room **FACING PAGE** The dining area is open-plan to the kitchen. The kitchen island was painted blue to match the ceiling lights

**BELOW** The master bedroom's silk shams and throw are from The White Company. 'Everyone who sees the bed says they want to dive into it,' says Maggie **RIGHT** The spare room bed was bought in a French flea market **BELOW RIGHT** Modern fittings and tiles make a sleek master bathroom

Maggie Beasley, husband Keith and Maggie's daughter, Klara, are quite the home makeover team. Although Maggie recently retired, she previously worked in kitchen design; Keith is a retired carpenter and had installed kitchens alongside Maggie for 26 years, and Klara has been working as an interior designer for the last 30 years. Friends thought Maggie and Keith were mad for retiring to a run-down 19th-century house in the Cotswolds that was, to put it mildly, a bit of a project. But with their experience in home improvement, and the interior design support they received from Klara, Hazel Cottage was always going to be in safe hands. Having taken the decision to downsize, the couple took a year to find the cottage, built in 1830. What appealed was its individuality – walls are thick, ceilings slope, windows are low, and room sizes irregular.

That's not to say Maggie didn't have doubts. 'When we moved in during April 2011 I did wonder why we'd bought it – it was so dark and dreary, and we'd worked on our previous home until it was perfect,' she says. 'But when you have specific ideas of what you want – as we did – you're never going to find somewhere that's 100 per cent right.'

When it came to renovating the cottage, the kitchen was obviously a top priority. Maggie knew she didn't want anything twee – though she wanted it to be in keeping with the house's history. White-painted wooden units

and original exposed brick teamed with blue industrial-style light fittings give an effect that's more New York loft than Cotswold cottage. Keith built shelving for the living room, kitchen and office – details where it pays to have a carpenter in the house. The couple redecorated throughout and enlisted builders to reconfigure the top floor (creating an en suite and moving the main bathroom).

Downsizing to a very different property –their previous house was 1960s – meant a lot of the couple's old furnishings didn't sit well here. Maggie kept an eye out for items to complement Klara's muted colour scheme. A favourite is the dining area's Edwardian dresser, rescued from a dental surgery under renovation. It cost £100, was restored by Keith, and painted by Maggie. Upstairs, a flea market bed, recovered in Andrew Martin fabric by Klara, takes centre stage in the spare room.

And does Maggie still wonder why they bought the cottage? Absolutely not. 'The downsize has brought us more financial security,' she says. 'Plus, it's a lovely home. I especially love being here in the winter – having the wood-burning stove on in the living room is wonderful. It's a superb focal point and is just so comforting.' And, not to downplay the financial implications – Maggie admits it's great for the heating bills, too. ∎
*To find out more about Klara's work, visit klaragoldy.co.uk*

# *Get the look*
# FRENCH

*Give your home a façade of laid-back elegance; mix a muted colour palette with grand furnishings and effortless details*

*Stylist's* PICK

1 'Megan' chandelier, £145, Chandelier and Mirror Company 2 Tigris lamp, £145, Oka 3 'Camille' carved armchair, £1,500, Sweetpea and Willow 4 White window mirror, £185, Cox and Cox 5 Red gingham cushion, from £14.13 each, Rooms You Love 6 'L'Ile des lanterns' wallpaper, £69 per roll, Zoffany 7 Double drawer worktable, £1,825, John Lewis of Hungerford 8 Upholstered bed, £1,410, Sweetpea and Willow 9 Set of 2 'Fleur de Lys' birdcages, £49.95, Dotcomgiftshop 10 Lisbeth Dahl candlestick, £14.99, Mollie and Fred 11 Dartington Crystal decanter, £95, John Lewis 12 'Camille' dusty blue quilt, £100, Berry Red ✤ *For stockist information see page 130*

# 20th-century style

*In these interiors, unfussy schemes let the
beautiful mid-century furniture do the talking*

**KATIE HALLETT**,
HOMES EDITOR

**Characterised by rich,** warm-hued woods and
organic, simplistic forms, it's not hard to see why
the popularity of mid-century furniture shows
no signs of waning. Those who have fallen for its
charms, have fallen hard and the homes in this
section are all a masterclass in creating a stylish look
– wherever you live. Wary of her home looking too
'themey', Helle Moyna has mixed 1960s and 1970s
Danish pieces with contemporary items while Rosie
Ames has contrasted her furnishings with paintings
and fabrics from her home country, South Africa.
These homeowners caught onto the look ahead of
the trend and many pieces were bought cheaply
from auction but, for an instant fix, pieces by top
mid-century names can be found at the Mid-
Century Modern Shows and Danish Homestore.

# Danish delights

*When Helle Moyna moved to this Battersea house,
she brought a slice of her home country with her...*

FEATURE **KATIE HALLETT** PHOTOGRAPHS **RACHEL WHITING**

**FACING PAGE, CLOCKWISE FROM FAR LEFT** Helle Moyner lives here with her husband David and two sons, Tobias and Marcus; the fireplace was made by Chesney's and is a replica of the original design; a photo of the sky by The Day That, taken on the day that Tobias was born, is displayed above a chest of drawers bought from Midcentury Modern. The vases are by Casalinga **THIS PAGE** Helle bought the bergère armchairs in the living room on the Danish auction website Lauritz 15 years ago and reupholstered them in a striking turquoise. The cushions are from By Nord Copenhagen and the coffee table is a vintage design by Grete Jalk, also bought at auction

*'I've always loved mixing old and new but, rather than going in the shabby chic direction, I prefer a more streamlined look '*

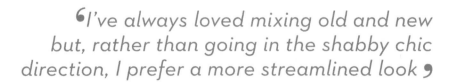

**CLOCKWISE FROM TOP LEFT** A Boffi kitchen creates a sleek feel in the kitchen. The stool is from an antiques shop on Church Street in London; the light-filled kitchen extension contains the family dining area. The chairs are Arne Jacobsen's 'Series 7' and the oak dining table was a wedding present; the pencil drawings in the en suite were found at local markets; a 1950s teak Hans Olsen rocking chair and 1960s table by Georg Jensen for Kubus add warmth to a corner of the living room. Both were bought from auction website Lauritz; Helle bought the rosewood sideboard at auction especially to fit this space in the living room **FACING PAGE** Muted blues, dark wood and hints of gold keep the master bedroom calm. The brass lamps are from Zara Home

S leek organic shapes, richly hued timbers, solid construction – who doesn't love a bit of mid-century Danish? For Danish-born Helle Moyna, it's a style that's always had a firm place in her home. 'I love the simple form and brilliant craftsmanship of pieces from that era and have bought a lot of mid-century pieces over the years, mostly from Danish auctions,' she says.

Prices for mid-century furniture have boomed with its popularity but when Helle bought many of her pieces, it was still affordable. Amazingly, the rosewood sideboard cost just £250. 'People have offered to buy it from me for £4,000,' she says. 'I always tell them that it's not for sale as it's one of my favourite pieces. I love how it fits so neatly into the space next to the fireplace: the builders who I asked to move it for me (it weighs a ton) didn't believe that it was the right size but there's a centimetre to spare either side.'

Helle has teamed older pieces with contemporary designs, to stop the house becoming too 'themey'. It is these designs that she champions on her interiors website, Nordic Elements. 'I've always loved mixing old and new but, rather than going in the shabby chic direction, I prefer a more streamlined look.'

The architecture of Helle's house, which she shares with husband David and sons Tobias and Marcus, certainly helps strike a sleek silhouette. The ceilings are high, rooms spacious and windows large – features that attracted Helle

and David from the get-go. 'When we moved here the walls were painted in shiny gloss, the floorboards were stained with a checkerboard pattern and the kitchen was tiny. It was definitely not our style but we loved the proportions.'

The couple got the keys, painted everything in (many) coats of Dulux's 'Antique White' and patiently planned what work needed to be done. The biggest project was the kitchen extension, which was built on to the side return. 'The previous kitchen was a mess, with absolutely no work space, but in a way this was good – it meant that we didn't feel guilty about ripping everything out and starting completely afresh.' That they did. The floors are now black slate, units are stainless steel-topped Boffi numbers and incredibly light thanks to sky-lights that run the length of the extension.

Elsewhere in the house, a spare bedroom was converted into a spacious en suite, windows were replaced, floorboards upgraded and walls replastered. The crumbling original fireplace in the living room was also replaced with a Chesney's number as it would have cost more to repair the existing design.

Although it sounds like an extensive list, Helle took the project in her stride. 'My dad was forever doing work around the house when I was growing up so putting my own stamp on a property comes naturally to me' she says. 'Everyone in Denmark is DIY crazy.' ■

*To find out more about Nordic Elements, visit nordicelements.co.uk*

# A place to call home

*Having moved more than 15 times in 20 years, renovating as she went along, architect Cat Martin seems surprisingly settled in her Bristol home*

FEATURE **ANGELA LINFORTH** PHOTOGRAPHS **JASON INGRAM**

**FACING PAGE, LEFT** Homeowner and architect Cat in her garden **FACING PAGE, RIGHT** The table is by Jean Nouvel. The fitted element of the kitchen is just the three grey units **THIS PAGE** The sofa is by Antonio Citterio by Flexform. The 'Mac Gee' shelving unit is by Philippe Starck and can collapse to be transported, and the table was bought in the local Habitat closing down sale

**ABOVE** Cat bought her world map wallpaper from travel specialists Stanfords. She put it on a foam board backing and can now use it as a pinboard for travel mementoes such as currency and postcards **FACING PAGE** The picture above the fireplace was picked up in a junk shop in London and turned out to be an Ivan Picelj original

'This is pretty much the longest I've lived anywhere since leaving home and it's interesting that I seem to be staying'

Y ou might expect an architect who has a passion for simplicity and an eye for detail to settle in a minimal glass box of their own design. Not so for Cat Martin, although that was the original plan. 'I wanted to move to Bristol and I'd just been gazumped on a fabulous top floor flat. This house was under offer when the agents called me and said that it had fallen though. I saw it and thought, "I could live here."'

Over six years later and Cat is still in situ, an extraordinary feat in itself for someone who has had more than 15 different addresses in the last 20 years on two different continents. Could it be that she's found her 'forever home'? 'This is pretty much the longest I've lived anywhere since leaving home and it's interesting that I seem to be staying. As an architect, the next project is always on the horizon. I just don't know when.'

Since her home is Grade II-listed and was built in 1840, this wasn't a project. But, explains Cat, that has proved to be surprisingly relaxing. 'Oddly, I like the fact that I can't do anything with it, as it means I'm not constantly thinking of improvements. I'm living with all the existing details. In my job I worry about the details all the time. Having lived in my own ruthlessly designed spaces, thinking

things like "I wish I'd done that skirting board detail differently", it's surprisingly restful living in a house where somebody else has made all the decisions.'

Although when it came to furnishing, Cat's attention to detail (or, more specifically, the details) is certainly acute. The search for a sofa took two years before she finally decided. Primarily though, she already had most of the contents, which she has been collecting since she started work as an architect. Her first piece, the Le Corbusier 'LC2' sofa, sits in the kitchen and reflects her taste for design classics. 'I collect pieces that are innovative in their use of material. It's easy to forget that a sheet of flexible plywood or steel tubing were once very different.'

The other factor that attracted Cat to her collection is portability as she's travelled across the world and back. Having worked for a decade in London for Richard Rogers and then for Hopkins (the Velodrome architects), she seized the opportunity to build houses in Australia. 'There's a very different approach to architecture there – clients aren't bogged down by such a sense of history. Also, with the blue sky, big windows and beaches, the homes are very photogenic.' The same could well be said of her Victorian home in weather-challenged Bristol. ∎
*Martin Architects can be contacted via martinarchitects.co.uk*

*'Oddly, I like the fact that you can't do anything with it, it means I'm not constantly looking for improvements. It's surprisingly restful'*

**CLOCKWISE FROM TOP LEFT** After trying a brilliant white in the bedroom, Cat switched to 'French Grey' by Little Greene. Then, after much deliberation, she opted for a lime green carpet. An orange throw, bought from The Conran Shop, completes the look; the bath was painted red; Cat's gradually collected the prints on the stairway, starting at age 16; the sculpture is by Alastair Mackie

# A slower pace

*Rosie and David Ames decided to trade in life in London for one in the depths of Devon – and in doing so, restored a roomy 1970s home*

FEATURE **KATIE HALLETT** PHOTOGRAPHS **RACHEL WHITING**

**CLOCKWISE FROM TOP LEFT** The couple fitted rubber flooring around the edge of the kitchen. The units are from Ikea and the lamp from John Lewis; a range cooker and stainless steel shelves lend an industrial edge to the kitchen; the beautiful seven-stem vase was handmade by David; the teak chair in the corner of the living room was bought for just £6 from a local charity shop; The dining table and bureau were both made by David **FACING PAGE** the Danish coffee table was bought from a Sue Ryder shop for just £11

**ABOVE** In the bathroom, the couple have opted for a marble, panelled bath and traditional sink **TOP** The couple reinstated a mid-century feel in the entrance hall by cladding the existing spindle staircase banister and topping with a piece of mahogany **RIGHT** Gentle lilac walls keep the mood restful in the guest bedroom

Tucked away down a steep rough track, one mile from the South Molton village of Romansleigh, it's fair to say that you wouldn't stumble across Rosie and David Ames's home by chance. And, for a house set so deeply in the countryside, a 1970s building is perhaps the opposite of what you might expect to find. 'We weren't looking for somewhere modern at all,' admits Rosie, 'When we started house-hunting we dreamt of a Devon longhouse with an Aga but this place ticked all the boxes: there aren't any near neighbours and the setting is beautiful, within 10 acres of land. We thought it would be an interesting adventure!'

'Being a 1970s house, it wasn't the best quality of build originally and it had become very run down,' says Rosie, who was born in Kenya. 'The chap who lived here before had tried to create a cottage feel inside – stripping away all the original features and replacing them with cheap off-the-shelf fittings. As we were downsizing we couldn't afford to throw lots of money at it – we had to be careful,' says Rosie. And so, the couple boxed in the staircase spindles and fitted a mahogany banister and opted for reclaimed floorboards.

The garden was a bit of a shocker, too – so overgrown that weeds obstructed the views from the downstairs windows. Rosie took charge of getting rid of

stinging nettles, rows of Leylandii and re-laying the vegetable patch – an essential element when living somewhere so remote. 'I never had a plan for the garden as such, it just evolved,' she says.

When the couple moved to Romansleigh they brought with them Rosie's Victorian furniture and David's more contemporary items – styles that had both fitted neatly into their Edwardian home in London. This wasn't the case here though. 'In the end we had to let the house dictate how we furnished it,' says Rosie. The couple scoured local charity shops and recycling centres and found unbelievable bargains: the beautiful coffee table in the living room was bought for £11 and teak chairs were a snip at £6 each. Even the Ercol chairs in the kitchen were picked up for just a couple of pounds.

There are other, more personal, influences around the house, too. Items brought back from South Africa, where Rosie has friends and family, remind her of home and the large, airy rooms provide the perfect setting for David's handsome furniture (he works as a cabinet-maker). Despite a few difficult winters the couple have adapted well to life in the country. 'I was brought up in the wilds of Africa,' says Rosie. 'So moving here was a bit like coming home. I love it.' ■
*If you'd like to rent Romansleigh for short periods, visit uniquehomestays.com*

# Get the look
# 20TH CENTURY

*Get your hands on a piece of modern history; these accessories mix mid-century cool with all the comforts of a well-lived-in home*

*Stylist's* PICK

1 'Cleo' bookcase, £150, Habitat 2 2-seater sofa, £599, Kubrick 3 Roberts Revival DAB radio, £199.99, John Lewis 4 'Poshly Polished' bedside table, £159, The French Bedroom Company 5 Krenit bowl, £16, Not on the High Street 6 John Hanly throw, £140, Liberty London 7 'The Beck Chair', £695, The East London Design Store 8 Cushion, £21, Bespo 9 'Twiitter' table lamp, £150, Heals 10 'Antelope' chair, £505, The Conran Shop ✤ *For stockist information see page 130*

# English eclectic

*These homes are proof that a little experimenting can result in some truly spectacular interiors*

**KATIE HALLETT,**
HOMES EDITOR

**The interior designer** responsible for reimagining a dated 15th-century cottage in Cornwall into an achingly cool family home didn't have a plan when he began bidding on pieces for the house at auction. Before long he had amassed a curious collection of pieces, including a mustard velvet sofa, a cartographer's ruler and a trio of fungus specimens. This pulling together of seemingly bonkers objects results in something rather special, as the homes in this chapter show. The look is dependent on having great vision for how pieces will look in different environments (think dark, brooding paint colours and quirky wallpapers) and the patience to scour auction catalogues, antiques shops and even charity shops for those pieces that most wouldn't dream of giving a second glance.

# Family affair

*Jacqui Brooks has her grandmothers to thank for her love of beautiful design – and her wonderfully eclectic home*

FEATURE **KATIE HALLETT** PHOTOGRAPHS **RACHEL WHITING**

**LEFT** Jacqui Brooks lives here with daughters Amelia (left) and Hollie (right)
**ABOVE** Jacqui stores her quilting fabrics in a cupboard that she distressed

'I bought the big Vernon Ward flower print from a charity shop for £11 a few years ago because it reminded me of my grandmother. It was the start of my collection of Ward pictures, bought from eBay and auctions,' says Jacqui

'*For me, memories make a home –
be they objects passed down from family
members, gifts from loved ones or simply
items that remind you of a holiday*'

**LEFT** The kitchen cupboards have
been painted in Little Greene's 'Salix'.
'I bought the Ercol table over 30 years
ago – it was my first kitchen table,'
says Jacqui **ABOVE** Jacqui finds many
of the window and swan vases from
charity shops **RIGHT** Amelia made
the bowl when she was at school

Jacqui Brooks is toying with the idea of extending into her attic. Not because she wants a guest room or to enlarge the size of the bedrooms but because the family business has gradually begun to take over the 1920s, Leicester home that she shares with her two daughters Hollie and Amelia. The trio launched MiaFleur, an online homeware boutique with a vintage focus, just over a year ago and, although the set-up sounds too good to be true, it's something that Jacqui has dreamt about for as long as she can remember.

'My paternal grandmother was a fine seamstress who made all her own clothes and soft furnishings and taught me to sew during my summer holidays, while my maternal grandmother's home was a treasure trove of beautiful objects and textiles,' she explains. 'They inspired me to forge a career in design – it was something that they would have loved for themselves.'

Before launching the business just over a year ago, Jacqui's job was far less glam, working full-time for the family potato merchants business. But, when Amelia graduated with a degree in textile design (and Hollie already had a degree in fashion and textile management under her belt) they decided it was time to go for it. The influence of Jacqui's grandmothers can be spotted throughout her home. The flower paintings in the garden room were collected because they reminded her of the designs owned by her maternal grandmother, while the brass and wood clock in the living room was one of the few things saved from her paternal grandmother's bungalow when it was flooded. 'For me, memories make a home,' says Jacqui. 'Be it objects passed down from family members, gifts from

loved ones or simply items that remind you of a holiday. That way, every time you look around, you're reminded of happy times.'

Rather than being tied to a particular era, Jacqui is drawn to colour and form and has a weakness for anything old or beautifully made. 'I prefer to buy vintage or items crafted by designer-makers as I love their individuality,' she says. 'I like things to have a story, even if I don't know what it is.'

Jacqui's most treasured belongings may speak of the past but this isn't to say she isn't afraid to take risks. When she moved here two years ago the house had been done up to sell – fireplaces were boarded up, the kitchen units were white gloss and the walls were all white. Needless to say, this wasn't quite her style. Rooms have gradually been given the MiaFleur treatment – statement floral wallpapers from Designers Guild and John Morris are juxtaposed with yet more florals in the upstairs rooms, while the family bathroom is painted in a dramatic black. A few months ago Jacqui made the brave move to paint the living room in Little Greene's brooding 'Scree', which had only been launched a few days before. 'For me, interior design is an organic process. I go with my gut,' she says.

Hollie and Amelia have adopted Jacqui's love for design in the same way that she adopted her grandmothers', and although this does come in handy when working together, it does mean that shopping trips can be tricky. 'Antiques shopping with my girls can feel a little bit like the Boxing Day sales,' says Jacqui. 'We all love the same things, so it's a race to snap up the best bits. There are a few coin tosses and trade-offs that come into play!' ∎

*For more information on MiaFleur, visit miafleur.com*

**THIS PAGE** The lamp on the Sweetpea & Willow bedside table was made by designer-maker Ami Derbyshire. 'I particularly love her work because she encapsulates old and new by making moulds from old pieces and then putting her own twist on them,' says Jacqui **FACING PAGE, CLOCKWISE FROM FAR LEFT** The silk cushion on the yellow chair was made by Scottish textile designer Emily Rose. It can be bought from MiaFleur; the oriental cabinet was given to Jacqui by her parents. She painted and distressed the lamp base and put fringing on the shade; the plate is by Anna Collette Hunt and was bought at the Great Northern Contemporary Craft Fair. The little bowl and spoon are by Claire Baker

# The best of both worlds

*The owners of Ledbury interiors store Tinsmiths have decorated their home with suitable rigour – vibrant fabrics and quirky accessories aplenty*

FEATURE **ANGELA LINFORTH** PHOTOGRAPHS **IAIN KEMP**

**FACING PAGE, LEFT** The sitting room is a glorious mass of rugs, cushions, walls full of prints, and collections of objects **FACING PAGE, RIGHT** Phoebe Clive lives here with her architect husband Alex and their two children Felix and Cyrus **THIS PAGE** Layers of pattern and colour in the form of quilts and cushion covers, prints and paintings on the walls, and even the rugs on the floor give a rich feel to the home

The fireplace in the living room was made from three old stone windowsills sourced from the couple's favourite salvage yard, Posterity, just outside Ledbury

...nks was added around 1780 **ABOVE** The top of the building houses the guest bedroom. It had been the previous owner's workshop **RIGHT** 'I think these little Chinese boxes are both decorative and captivating with their funny little scenes,' says Phoebe

*'When you visit a town, you don't imagine what it's like above or behind the shops. Going up the alleyway from the main street was like opening a whole other world'*

With a 30-second commute to work in the centre of Ledbury, it's easy to imagine that Alex and Phoebe Clive's home would be a non-stop bustle of noise and activity. Not so. Despite being on the Herefordshire market town's main strip, the Tudor-period house with its sunny roof terrace is tranquillity itself. It's also large (three storeys) with few of the constraints that living in the centre of town normally brings. At the back, there is not only parking but enough space to build both a steel structure to run a business, as well as keep chickens – which is handy as the countryside was the couple's stomping ground before they made their wholly unexpected move in 2004.

'It was curiosity that brought me to the house but, once I'd seen it, I thought it was amazing,' says Phoebe. 'When you visit a town, you don't imagine what the living spaces are like above or behind the shops. Going up the alleyway from the main street to the house was like opening a whole other world. I thought at the time, "Buying this place is going to be the best thing that we've ever done," and it was.'

The house didn't just bring living accommodation for the couple and their son Felix but also a whole new way of life for Phoebe. She is the owner of one of

H&A's favourite shops, Tinsmiths – a veritable trove of fabulous fabrics, prints, lighting, furniture, utility glassware and the sort of interiors accessories that you simply don't see elsewhere. 'I wanted a shop that would be more than a hobby and would do a bit more than just pay some bills,' she says.

Tinsmiths started small in 2004 as the only retailer outside London to stock rolls of Ian Mankin's covetable tickings along with a carefully selected range of UK-made interiors accessories. The shop grew rapidly, a website was launched and, when Alex completed the steel structure, instead of renting it out, which had been the plan, Tinsmiths spread up the garden path and moved in.

When it came to the house, there was little doubt that its contents would be 'pre-loved'. A childhood spent in the auction rooms of Norfolk has left Phoebe with an appetite for seeking out unusual finds. 'My mum was a bric-a-braccy sort of dealer during the Seventies and loved making curtains. Consequently, I spent a lot of my childhood sitting on market stalls sewing curtains, an experience that has proved to be terribly handy.' While the shop and the home are very different, they are united by a strong love of innovative, appealing design. ∎

*For more information on Tinsmiths, visit shop.tinsmiths.co.uk*

# Entertaining
## *eccentricity*

*Two miles from Weymouth beach, Narda and Tris Harris have brought out the warmth and cosiness of their 17th-century home*

FEATURE **KATIE HALLETT** PHOTOGRAPHS **DAVID PARMITER**

**FACING PAGE** Narda and Tris Harris love spending their weekends at the cottage with their dog, Biscuit **THIS PAGE** Narda and Tris designed the kitchen themselves, furnishing it with pieces bought from JS Auctions near Bicester, a Lacanche cooker and Ercol kitchen chairs found on eBay

*'I like to think of the look we've gone for as English eccentric – it's chintz with attitude!'*

As Narda and Tris Harris drive down the country lane, towards their holiday home in Weymouth, Dorset, the couple's fox terrier, Biscuit, becomes very excited. 'When we go over the speed bumps she can sense that we're approaching the cottage,' says Narda. 'We can empathise – she loves spending time here as much as we do. The house is our absolute passion.'

The couple spent a month of scouring Wiltshire, Somerset and Dorset before they came across the 17th-century cottage, just two miles from the coastal town of Weymouth. 'We hadn't been to Dorset before and didn't know anything about the area but I've always wanted a big garden, as I love gardening, and Tris had always dreamed of living by the sea, so the cottage gives us the best of both worlds,' says Narda. The couple love hosting big family gatherings but the house only had a narrow galley kitchen when they moved in, making it difficult to entertain. To rectify this they employed a builder to live in the house for six months while he transformed the granny annexe, raising the ceiling and changing the layout to hold the roomy kitchen, extra bedroom and en suite.

Narda was determined to maintain the country feel of the house and in terms of decorating, changed the cool coastal shades for warm reds and greens. 'Because it's an old cottage it screamed out to be cosy,' she says. 'I like to think of the look we've gone for as English eccentric – chintz with attitude!' As a result the beamed master bedroom is papered in toile de Jouy and furnished with dark wood modern pieces while the sitting room has a gentleman's library feel with its tartan fabrics, chesterfield sofa and roaring open fire.

As the sister of *Flog it!* expert Michael Baggott, Narda has antiques in the blood. 'One of the biggest bargains in the house is the kitchen furniture. Before we'd completed on the house we went to a big auction and ended up buying the kitchen table and four dressers. We were tempting fate as we wouldn't have had anywhere to put them if the sale fell through!' Other decorative pieces in the house, such as the wooden elephants in the sitting room, were donated by Michael. 'I'm very lucky to have a brother who's in the business. He'll buy a box of items from auction, keep the one thing he likes and give the rest to us.' ■

**CLOCKWISE FROM TOP LEFT** The collection of convex mirrors in the hallway were cheaply sourced from various antiques shops; the guest bedroom is decorated with Cole & Son 'Hummingbirds' wallpaper; *Toile de Jouy* wallpaper and curtains by Manuel Canovas are loyal to the traditional feel of the cottage, especially when paired with the original beams; the main bathroom is painted in soothing 'Old White' by Farrow & Ball **FACING PAGE, TOP** Narda and Tris have created a cosy feel in the sitting room with Manuel Canovas wallpaper and a Seventies chair recovered in Colefax and Fowler fabric **FACING PAGE, BOTTOM** The mirror and metal table in the sun room are from Ginko Gardens in Hammersmith

# *Relax and unwind*

*Ken Aylmer has created a warm but quirky holiday home for his family in the middle of the Cornish countryside*

FEATURE **KATIE HALLETT** PHOTOGRAPHS **JASON INGRAM**

**FACING PAGE, LEFT** The Aylmer family: Illona, Scarlet, Ella, Leo and Ken stand on the grounds of Tregulland **FACING PAGE, RIGHT** White rendering on the walls has been stripped back to expose what used to be the exterior wall of the cottage **THIS PAGE** The 'Granary' living room, in the 18th-century barn, is much loved by Ken. One of the beams hides a pull-down cinema screen for film nights. The coffee table was made by Footprint Joinery and the sofa is a secondhand B&B Italia number

The legs of the dining table were taken from telegraph poles

# Save 50%

when you subscribe to *Homes & Antiques* magazine today

12 issues of Homes & Antiques

for just £23*

## YOUR SPECIAL SUBSCRIBER PACKAGE

* **Save a fantastic 50%** on the shop price*

* Just **£23 every 12 issues** when you pay by Direct Debit

* Enjoy **exclusive subscriber-only pages** every quarter

* Receive every issue direct to your door with **FREE UK delivery**

* **Never miss an issue** of your favourite magazine

Please quote
**HAVBKZ14**

## SUBSCRIBE ONLINE TODAY AT
**buysubscriptions.com/homesandantiques/HAVBKZ14**

OR CALL OUR ORDER HOTLINE ON **0844 844 0255†**

†Lines open Monday to Friday 8am to 8pm and Saturday 9am to 1pm. Calls to this number from a BT landline will cost no more than 5p per minute. Calls from any other providers may vary.